Kamala Harris

THIS EDITION

Produced for DK by WonderLab Group LLC
Jennifer Emmett, Erica Green, Kate Hale, *Founders*

Editor Maya Myers; **Photography Editor** Nicole DiMella; **Managing Editor** Rachel Houghton;
Designers Project Design Company; **Researcher** Michelle Harris; **Copy Editor** Lori Merritt;
Indexer Connie Binder; **Proofreader** Susan K. Hom; **Series Reading Specialist** Dr. Jennifer Albro

First American Edition, 2025
Published in the United States by DK Publishing, a division of Penguin Random House LLC
1745 Broadway, 20th Floor, New York, NY 10019

A catalog record for this book is available from the Library of Congress.
HC ISBN: 979-8-2171-2542-5
PB ISBN: 979-8-2171-2541-8

DK books are available at special discounts when purchased in bulk for sales promotions, premiums, fund-raising, or educational use.
For details, contact:
DK Publishing Special Markets, 1745 Broadway, 20th Floor, New York, NY 10019
SpecialSales@dk.com

Printed and bound in Canada
Super Readers Lexile® levels 620L to 790L
Lexile® is the registered trademark of MetaMetrics, Inc. Copyright © 2024 MetaMetrics, Inc. All rights reserved.

The publisher would like to thank the following for their kind permission to reproduce their images:
a=above; c=center; b=below; l=left; r=right; t=top; b/g=background
Alamy Stock Photo: Abaca Press / Yuri Gripas 31b, American Photo Archive / Official White House Photo by Lawrence Jackson 2,
Archivio GBB 8, 9, 11, 13, 14, 16tr, Associated Press / George Nikitin 17, DOD Photo / Planetpix 12, Geopix / Biden for President / Adam
Shultz 34t, Media Punch / Faye Sadou 39tr, MediaPunch Inc 30, PBH 24, Pictorial Press Ltd 27t, lev radin 43t, UPI / Kevin Dietsch 36tr,
ZUMA Press, Inc. / Eric Slomanson 22, ZUMA Press, Inc. / Justin L. Stewart 33; **Getty Images:** AFP / Jim Watson 36b, Bloomberg /
Hannah Beier 45, Jon Cherry 37, Kevin Dietsch 27br, Andrew Harnik 35, HUM Images / Universal Images Group 25tr, MediaNews Group
/ Oakland Tribune / Howard Erker 10, MediaNews Group / The Mercury News / Gary Reyes 28-29t, MediaNews Group / The Mercury
News / Mary F. Calvert 19, San Francisco Chronicle / Hearst Newspapers / Christina Koci Hernandez 21, San Francisco Chronicle /
Hearst Newspapers / Kat Wade 25br, San Francisco Chronicle / Hearst Newspapers / Mike Kepka 20, San Francisco Chronicle / Hearst
Newspapers / Paul Chinn 23, The Washington Post / Matt McClain 38clb; **Getty Images / iStock:** Jacob Wackerhausen 18;
Shutterstock.com: Dallasetta 15b, Maxim Elramsisy 42br, EQRoy 16b, Sheila Fitzgerald 32tr, Michael F. Hiatt 32, jayk67 15tl, Dimitrios
Karamitros 34crb, Phil Mistry 1, lev radin 4-5, Carmen K. Sisson 42tr; **U.S. government works:** Official White House Photo by Adam
Schultz 26, 29br, 38-39t, 44, Official White House Photo by Chuck Kennedy 6, Official White House Photo by Lawrence Jackson 40bl,
40br, 41

Cover images: *Front:* **Dreamstime.com:** Les Cunliffe (flag); **U.S. government works:** Official White House Photo by Cameron Smith;
Back: **Dreamstime.com:** Redhotvector cra, Olena Zhuravska cl

www.dk.com

MIX
Paper | Supporting
responsible forestry
FSC™ C018179

This book was made with Forest
Stewardship Council™ certified
paper — one small step in DK's
commitment to a sustainable future.
Learn more at www.dk.com/uk/
information/sustainability

Kamala Harris

Sarah Fuentes

Contents

Harris being sworn in as VP in January 2021

"I may be the first woman to hold this office. But I won't be the last."

—Kamala Harris

Madam Vice President

Kamala Harris is an American politician and attorney. Her journey into politics is one of resilience and perseverance. Her career has demonstrated her commitment to justice, equality, and service.

Harris is a woman of many firsts. She was the first woman, first Black American, and first South Asian American to become attorney general of California. She was the first South Asian American and second Black woman to become a US senator. And on January 20, 2021, Kamala Harris made history as the first woman, first Black American, and first South Asian American to serve as vice president of the United States of America.

Kamala Harris is an inspiration to people around the world. In her success, many young people see the possibility of achieving their own dreams.

Daughter of Immigrants

Kamala Devi Harris was born on October 20, 1964, in Oakland, California. Her parents were both immigrants to the United States. Her mother, Shyamala Gopalan, was born in Chennai, India. Her father, Donald Harris, was born in Jamaica.

Both Shyamala and Donald came to America to continue their education. They met as students in California. Shyamala was studying to become a scientist. Donald was studying economics.

Shyamala and Donald on their wedding day, 1963

Kamala and Maya, 1968

Both Kamala's parents were civil rights activists. In 1963, they were married. Then, they became parents. Kamala was born in 1964, and in 1967, the family welcomed her sister, Maya. The girls were raised with a strong sense of justice and equality. Shyamala and Donald taught them that they could be anything if they worked hard.

Immigration

For hundreds of years, people from all over the world have come to the land we now call the United States. People immigrate to build new lives in another country. Immigrants bring languages, foods, fashions, and ideas to their new home. They help make America's culture diverse and vibrant.

A Wonderful Childhood

Kamala has fond memories of her youth. "I was very fortunate to have a really wonderful childhood," she has said. Her multicultural home celebrated a mix of American, Indian, and Jamaican customs and values.

Kamala's childhood was a time of change across the country. People were fighting for equality for all Americans. Kamala's parents stayed active in the civil rights movement. They brought baby Kamala to protest marches in her stroller. Even though she was young, these experiences deeply shaped her view of the world. She saw how important and challenging the movement for civil rights was.

A protest march in San Francisco, 1968

> "I believe it is an expression of patriotism to fight for the ideals of our country."
>
> —Kamala Harris

Kamala, 1967

As a kid, Kamala was confident and kind. Her parents taught her to use her voice to fight for justice and fairness.

As an adult, she would become committed to social justice. She believed in the promise of America for all Americans. She used her voice to create change. She wanted to help make the country better for all people.

Shyamala wanted her biracial daughters to understand their identity as Black women in America. She knew most people would see her daughters as Black first. The girls would face racism and unfair treatment. She wanted them to bond with other Black women and girls. They needed to learn to navigate the challenges that lay ahead.

Regina Shelton owned a daycare downstairs from Kamala's family's apartment. Kamala and Maya spent a lot of time there. Regina became like a second mother.

Gesture of Love

When Kamala was sworn in as senator and vice president, she placed her hand on Regina Shelton's family Bible. This was a gesture of gratitude to the woman who helped shape her life and career in public service.

"My mother... was determined to make sure we would grow into confident, proud Black women."

—Kamala Harris

Regina connected Kamala to her Black community. She brought Kamala to a Black church. She taught her how to cook soul food. She provided a nurturing environment and a sense of community. She showed Kamala the importance of giving back and serving others. Regina encouraged Kamala's commitment to public service.

Family Changes

In the late 1960s, Donald and Shyamala took jobs at a university in Illinois. The Harris family moved. Later, they moved to Wisconsin.

No matter where they lived, Kamala's life was filled with joy. She loved playing outdoors with her little sister. The family celebrated birthdays around the kitchen table.

When Kamala was seven years old, her parents divorced. Donald stayed in Wisconsin to teach. Shyamala returned to California with her daughters.

Kamala, 1979

Chennai, India

But Kamala stayed connected to both sides of her heritage. Shyamala took the girls to visit their grandparents in India. The girls also visited their father's family in Jamaica. Kamala embraced her identity as a biracial person in a multicultural family.

In 1976, Shyamala moved with her daughters to Montreal, Canada. Kamala attended Westmount High School. She was a hardworking student. She performed with a dance troupe. She earned money as a babysitter.

Westmount High School

Learning to Fight for Change

Kamala attended Vanier College in Montreal for one year. Then, she transferred to Howard University, a historically Black university in Washington, DC.

Kamala, 1986

At Howard, Kamala studied hard. She joined university groups, including student government and debate. She became a member of Alpha Kappa Alpha, a Black sorority. She graduated with a degree in political science and economics. Kamala was learning skills she'd need to become a leader.

Howard University

> **"Don't just sit around and complain about things. Do something."**
>
> —Shyamala Gopalan

Shyamala, at Harris's swearing in, 2004

All her life, Kamala had been taught to care for the rights of all people. She had spent years attending rallies with her mother. She had heard the voices of community leaders. She had overheard adults like her grandfather talking about politics. She had learned about the importance of justice.

Kamala was proud of her heritage. She wanted to give back to her community. She knew she would be a fighter for change.

Howard University

Howard University is one of the top HBCUs in the US. Howard was founded in 1867 to help Black students get an excellent education. Students of all backgrounds attend the school today. The university celebrates and embraces Black history and culture.

Prosecution and Defense

There are two basic types of trial lawyers: prosecuting attorneys (also called prosecutors) and defense attorneys. Prosecutors work to make sure that people who break the law are held responsible for their actions. A prosecutor investigates crimes and argues in court on behalf of the public. Defense attorneys defend people accused of crimes. They protect accused people's legal rights.

Kamala returned to California to attend what is now called the University of California College of the Law, San Francisco. In law school, Kamala continued to develop as a leader. She was president of the Black Law Students Association. She worked toward building diversity on campus.

In 1990, Kamala Harris began her career as a lawyer. Harris's first job was as a prosecutor in Alameda, California. She earned the job of deputy district attorney for the state of California. In this position, she represented the people of California. She took people and businesses that had been accused of crimes to court. She made sure that those who were guilty of crimes were held responsible.

"Lawyers have a profound ability and responsibility to be a voice for the vulnerable and the voiceless."

—Kamala Harris

Deputy DA Harris, 1997

Harris running for San Francisco DA, 2003

Harris was passionate about her job. Her work helped people in her community stay safe from serious crimes.

Growing up, Harris had seen how crime and injustice impacted her community. And she knew that the criminal justice system wasn't always fair. As a prosecutor, she believed she could make positive changes in the system. She hoped to change things from the inside. She wanted to make sure everyone was treated fairly. And she wanted to help keep the community safe.

In 2000, Harris took a new job at San Francisco City Hall. She was in charge of the Family and Children's Services Division. She prosecuted cases against people who hurt or neglected children.

Harris running for reelection as DA, 2007

Elected in San Francisco

In 2002, Harris ran for district attorney (DA) of San Francisco. She became the first person of color to win this job in the city.

As DA, Harris was tough on gun-related crimes. She created a team to focus on hate crimes against LGBTQ+ teens. Another team worked to stop environmental crimes. She created a program that helped keep people from returning to prison after they'd been released.

Harris learned that many criminals and victims of crimes had dropped out of school or skipped school a lot. To help keep kids in school, she made a rule that parents could be fined if their child missed a lot of school. Truancy rates dropped dramatically.

DA Harris in a courtroom, 2004

District Attorney

A district attorney is the top prosecutor for a county or district. A DA works with police officers and judges as part of the legal system. If a person breaks the law, the DA helps decide whether they should go to court. They work to ensure that the legal system is fair.

A Triple First for California

In 2010, Harris ran for California attorney general (AG). A state's AG helps enforce laws for the entire state. They also advise the state government on legal matters. When Harris won the election for AG, she became a triple first. She was the first woman AG of California, the first Black AG of California, and the first South Asian American AG of any state.

Maya Harris watching as her sister is sworn in for her second term as AG, 2011

> **"One of my mother's favorite sayings was, 'Don't let anybody tell you who you are. You tell them who you are.'"**
>
> —Kamala Harris

As AG, Harris won cases against large companies. She introduced the California Homeowner Bill of Rights. The bill made sure banks and other companies were fair. This helped people keep their homes. Harris also pushed for tech companies to protect customers' privacy. Her work as an AG helped protect citizens.

Heartbreaking Loss

In 2008, Harris's mother was diagnosed with colon cancer. After a career of work toward curing cancer, Shyamala battled her own cancer for a year. She died in 2009. Harris has called her mother "the greatest source of inspiration in my life."

Momala

In 2013, Harris's friends set her up on a blind date with a lawyer named Doug Emhoff. Emhoff was an entertainment lawyer. He was raised in a Jewish family. He had two teen children, Cole and Ella.

Harris and Emhoff fell in love. They were married on August 22, 2014. Kamala became stepmother to Cole and Ella. They lovingly call her Momala. "It's the name the kids gave me, and I wear it proudly," Harris has said.

Cole, Harris, Emhoff, and Ella

Family has always been important to Harris. She loves being a mom. She says of Cole and Ella, "They are brilliant, talented, funny kids who have grown into remarkable adults."

A Family Affair

Amara and Leela, Harris's grandnieces, spoke at the 2024 Democratic National Convention. They taught people how to pronounce their auntie's name. "First you say comma, like a comma in a sentence," Amara said. "Then you say la, like la la la la la," Leela said. Put it all together: Kama-la!

Representing California

In 2016, Harris decided to run for one of California's US Senate seats. During her campaign, Harris traveled all over the state to talk to voters. She promised to work for justice and equality. She pledged to help children and families. She promised to protect the environment and fight for healthcare.

Harris won her seat in the Senate with over 60 percent of the vote. She was sworn in as a senator in January 2017.

US Senate

A US senator is a member of the US Senate. There are 100 senators, two for each state. Senators discuss ideas for new laws, then vote to decide which ideas become laws. Along with the House of Representatives, the Senate helps make laws for the United States. A senator is elected for a six-year term.

"**Kamala Harris fights for us…. She'll be a fearless fighter for the people of California—all the people of California— every single day.**"

—Barack Obama, 2016

As a senator, Harris worked hard to create positive changes for American families. Many of the bills Harris sponsored and supported focused on civil rights, healthcare, and economic justice.

She cosponsored the Raise the Wage Act. This increased the minimum wage for workers nationwide. This meant families had more money for the things they needed, such as food and housing.

Senator Harris working with a committee in 2017

MS. HARF

Committee Work

Senators help make laws by serving on committees. These groups learn about different topics and recommend laws to the whole Senate. They also make sure government groups are doing their work correctly. Harris served on four important committees during her time in the Senate: budget, homeland security, intelligence, and judiciary.

Harris worked to make healthcare more easily available to all Americans. She supported a bill to lower the prices of prescription medication. She worked to make childcare available for families with working parents. She also continued to work toward reform in the criminal justice system.

A Candidate for the People

In January 2019, Harris announced she was running for president. Her campaign slogan was "For the People." She wanted to improve others' lives. During her campaign, Harris spoke about eliminating government support of private prisons. She talked about making family housing more affordable, increasing teacher pay, and much more.

Presidential Elections

Every four years, the US holds a national election to choose a new president. Usually, the two main candidates come from the Republican and Democratic parties. These are the two biggest political parties in the country. A president can serve no more than two four-year terms.

"I love my country...
I feel a sense of
responsibility to
fight for the best of
who we are."

—Kamala Harris, 2019

Twenty major candidates wanted to represent the Democratic Party. But only one would be chosen as the nominee. The Democratic nominee would be running against the Republican nominee: the president at the time, Donald J. Trump. Many Democrats thought Harris would be a strong contender against Trump. But in December, Harris made the difficult decision to end her first campaign for president. She would continue her work in the Senate.

VP Harris

A few months later, former Vice President Joseph R. Biden became the official Democratic nominee. Biden announced he would choose a woman as the vice-presidential candidate.

Electoral College
The Electoral College is a system used to pick the president of the United States. In most states, the candidate who gets the most individual votes in the state gets all of that state's electoral votes. The first candidate to get 270 electoral votes wins the election.

In August 2020, he chose Harris as his running mate. Biden and Harris were running against Trump and Vice President Mike Pence. After months of fierce campaigning, the race was very close. So close, in fact, that on Election Day, November 3, no winner was declared. Neither candidate had enough electoral votes to win yet.

For four days, Harris waited with the rest of the world for the election results. Then, on November 7, she was out for a jog with her husband. Her phone rang. It was Biden. He told her they had won.

Emhoff recorded the moment Harris picked up the phone. "We did it, Joe!" Harris said with a huge smile. "We did it!"

Insurrection

Two weeks before the inauguration, a large mob stormed the US Capitol building. They did not like the results of the election. Congress was meeting to officially count the votes, and the mob wanted to stop them. They did not succeed.

January 20, 2021, was Inauguration Day. Joe Biden became the 46th president of the United States. Kamala Harris became the vice president.

President Biden talked about unity, healing, and moving forward as a country. And VP Harris made history. She said that this moment showed the nation's character. "We not only see what has been, we see what can be."

vice president's residence

When Harris became vice president, she moved into the vice president's residence. This large house is at the US Naval Observatory in Washington, DC. Harris and Emhoff are the eighth vice-presidential family to live here.

An Author, Too
Kamala Harris has written three books. *Smart on Crime* and *The Truths We Hold* are nonfiction books. *Superheroes Are Everywhere* is a children's picture book.

Biden and Harris crossing the South Lawn of the White House, 2023

The president works in the White House's Oval Office. The VP's office is right across the street, in the Eisenhower Executive Office Building. During her time as VP, much of Harris's day was spent in the West Wing of the White House, where she worked closely with Biden.

As vice president, Harris worked to promote vaccination efforts and support the nation's recovery after the COVID-19 pandemic. She advocated for laws that helped protect people's ability to vote. She supported efforts to address climate change by promoting clean energy. She fought to improve Americans' access to healthcare.

Harris at Peterson Space Force Base, 2024

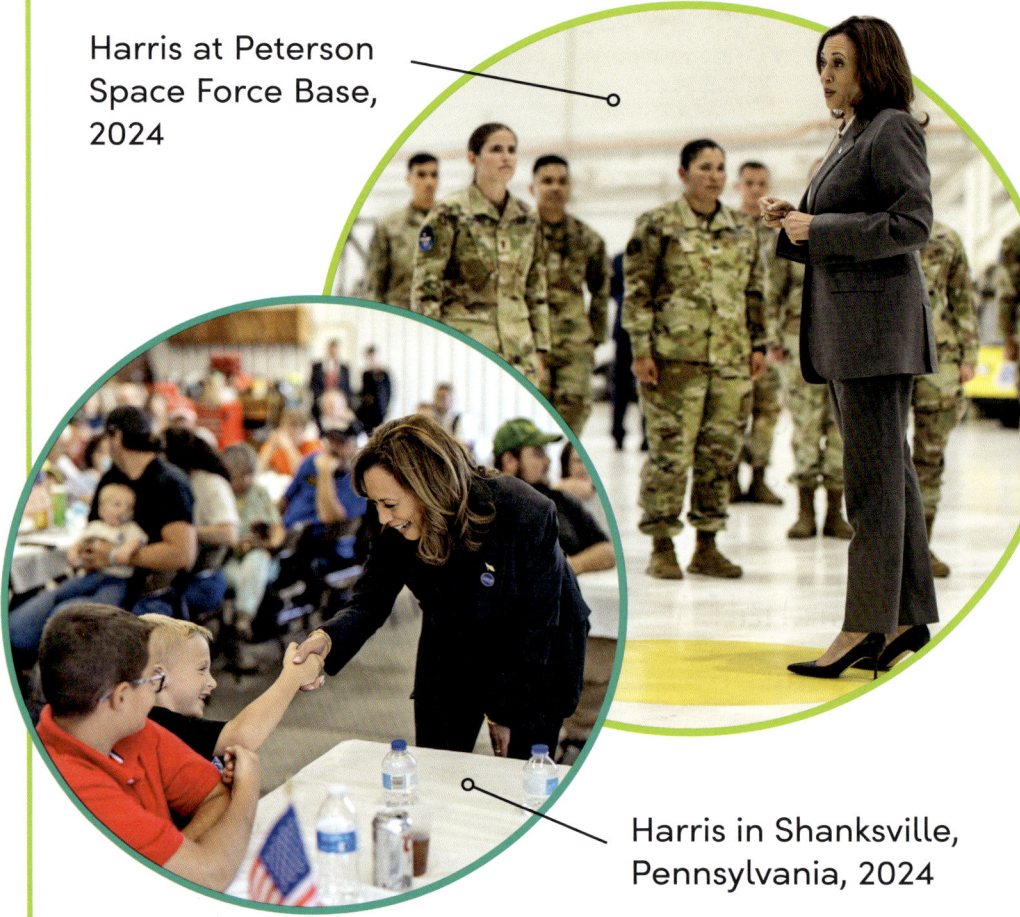

Harris in Shanksville, Pennsylvania, 2024

Harris meeting with Texas legislators, 2021

Harris also returned to the Senate floor sometimes. Because there are 100 senators, their votes on a bill or law can be split evenly in half. When the senators' votes are a 50-50 tie, the vice president steps in to cast the tie-breaking vote. Harris broke tied votes in the Senate many times as VP, more than any other VP in history.

Stepping Up to Lead

In 2024, Biden and Harris ran for reelection. Together, they asked people to vote for them to continue leading the country. They were running against former president Donald Trump, who picked JD Vance as his vice-presidential running mate.

However, in July 2024, Biden decided it was time for new leadership. On July 21, 2024, VP Kamala Harris announced her intention to run for president. She was quickly endorsed by Biden and others.

Harris chose Minnesota governor Tim Walz as her running mate. Harris and Walz traveled around the country to speak to the American people. They shared their vision for the future. Their campaign slogan was "We're not going back!"

The 2024 Democratic National Convention was held in Chicago, Illinois. People called delegates attend the convention. The delegates vote to officially pick their candidate. At the convention, Harris officially accepted the Democratic nomination for president.

Harris was the first woman of color to become a presidential nominee. Had she been elected, she would have been the first female president, the first South Asian American president, and the second Black president of the US.

Throughout her career, Kamala Harris has broken barriers, fought for justice, and paved the way for future generations of leaders. She inspires people to get involved, stay hopeful, and work for a better future.

Glossary

Biracial
Having parents of two different races

Campaign
An effort to get a person elected to a public office

Culture
The customary beliefs, traditions, values, and practices of a group of people

Delegate
A person who represents a larger group at a political convention

Economics
The study of how people use money and resources

Equality
Treatment that is the same for all people

HBCU
In the US, a historically Black college or university

Heritage
Traditions passed down through generations in a family

Justice
Fair treatment, or the righting of a wrong

Nominee
The person selected to represent a political party in an election

Politician
A person who works in government and helps to make laws

Political party
A group of people who agree on certain factors and work together to help direct government

Political science
The study of government, leadership, and lawmaking

Protest
To act, speak, or march in order to change something considered to be wrong

Racism
Believing in or giving unfair treatment based on race or skin color

Slogan
A phrase that helps people remember something important about a political candidate or a product

Truancy
Not going to school when you are supposed to

Index

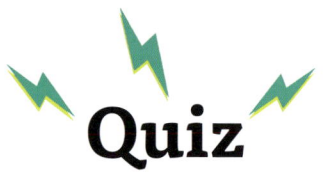

Quiz

Answer the questions to see what you have learned. Check your answers in the key below.

1. From which countries did Harris's parents immigrate?

2. In what state did Kamala Harris serve as attorney general?

3. When did Kamala Harris first run for president of the United States?

4. What historic achievement did Kamala Harris accomplish in 2021?

5. What year did Harris become the Democratic presidential nominee?

1. India and Jamaica 2. California 3. 2019 4. She became the first female VP, the first Black VP, and the first South Asian VP of the United States 5. 2024